VOL. 9

HAL•LEONARD®

GUITAR
PLAY-ALONG

AUDIO
ACCESS
INCLUDED

PLAYBACK+
Speed • Pitch • Balance • Loop

Easy ACOUSTIC SONGS

T0068351

ISBN 978-1-4950-4736-7

HAL•LEONARD®
CORPORATION
7777 W. BLUEMOUND RD. P.O. BOX 13819 MILWAUKEE, WI 53213

Visit Hal Leonard Online at
www.halleonard.com

GUITAR NOTATION LEGEND

THE MUSICAL STAFF shows pitches and rhythms and is divided by bar lines into measures. Pitches are named after the first seven letters of the alphabet.

TABLATURE graphically represents the guitar fingerboard. Each horizontal line represents a string, and each number represents a fret.

4th string, 2nd fret   1st & 2nd strings open, played together   open D chord

HALF-STEP BEND: Strike the note and bend up 1/2 step.

WHOLE-STEP BEND: Strike the note and bend up one step.

GRACE NOTE BEND: Strike the note and immediately bend up as indicated.

SLIGHT (MICROTONE) BEND: Strike the note and bend up 1/4 step.

BEND AND RELEASE: Strike the note and bend up as indicated, then release back to the original note. Only the first note is struck.

PRE-BEND: Bend the note as indicated, then strike it.

VIBRATO: The string is vibrated by rapidly bending and releasing the note with the fretting hand.

PALM MUTING: The note is partially muted by the pick hand lightly touching the string(s) just before the bridge.

HAMMER-ON: Strike the first (lower) note with one finger, then sound the higher note (on the same string) with another finger by fretting it without picking.

PULL-OFF: Place both fingers on the notes to be sounded. Strike the first note and without picking, pull the finger off to sound the second (lower) note.

LEGATO SLIDE: Strike the first note and then slide the same fret-hand finger up or down to the second note. The second note is not struck.

SHIFT SLIDE: Same as legato slide, except the second note is struck.

TRILL: Very rapidly alternate between the notes indicated by continuously hammering on and pulling off.

TAPPING: Hammer ("tap") the fret indicated with the pick-hand index or middle finger and pull off to the note fretted by the fret hand.

NATURAL HARMONIC: Strike the note while the fret-hand lightly touches the string directly over the fret indicated.

PINCH HARMONIC: The note is fretted normally and a harmonic is produced by adding the edge of the thumb or the tip of the index finger of the pick hand to the normal pick attack.

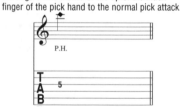

TREMOLO PICKING: The note is picked as rapidly and continuously as possible.

VIBRATO BAR DIVE AND RETURN: The pitch of the note or chord is dropped a specified number of steps (in rhythm), then returned to the original pitch.

VIBRATO BAR SCOOP: Depress the bar just before striking the note, then quickly release the bar.

VIBRATO BAR DIP: Strike the note and then immediately drop a specified number of steps, then release back to the original pitch.

Additional Musical Definitions

    (accent)   • Accentuate note (play it louder).

    (staccato)   • Play the note short.

D.S. al Coda   • Go back to the sign (𝄋), then play until the measure marked "*To Coda*," then skip to the section labelled "**Coda**."

D.C. al Fine   • Go back to the beginning of the song and play until the measure marked "*Fine*" (end).

Fill   • Label used to identify a brief melodic figure which is to be inserted into the arrangement.

N.C.   • Harmony is implied.

   • Repeat measures between signs.

   • When a repeated section has different endings, play the first ending only the first time and the second ending only the second time.

Hal•Leonard®
GUITAR
PLAY-ALONG

Easy ACOUSTIC SONGS

CONTENTS

The A Team

Words and Music by Ed Sheeran

*Symbols in parentheses represent chord names respective to capoed guitar.
Symbols above reflect actual sounding chords. Capoed fret is "0" in tab.

7

Good Riddance (Time of Your Life)

Words by Billie Joe
Music by Green Day

Interlude

Verse

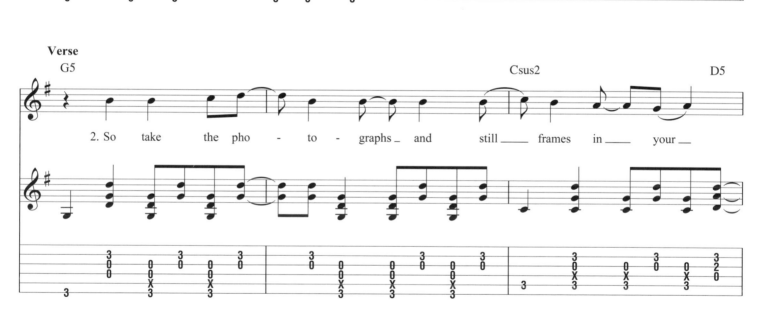

2. So take the pho - to - graphs _ and still _ frames in _ your _

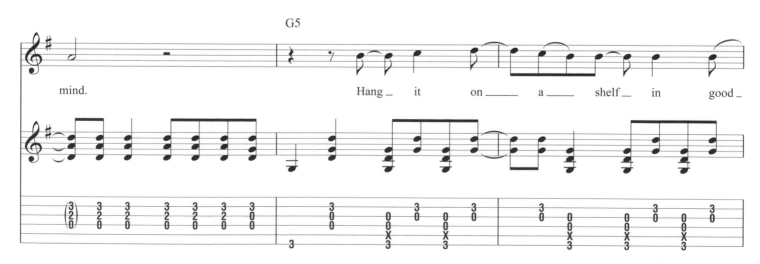

mind. Hang _ it on _ a _ shelf _ in good _

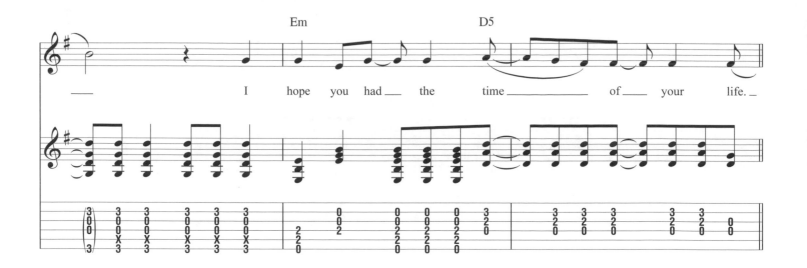

I hope you had ____ the time _____ of ____ your life. __

Interlude

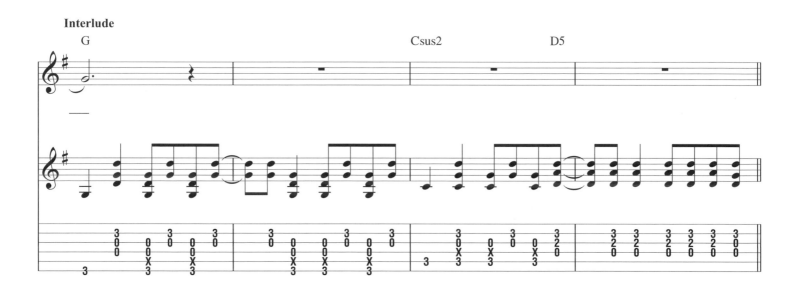

Play 3 times

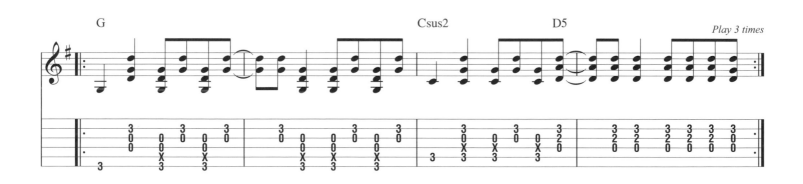

1.

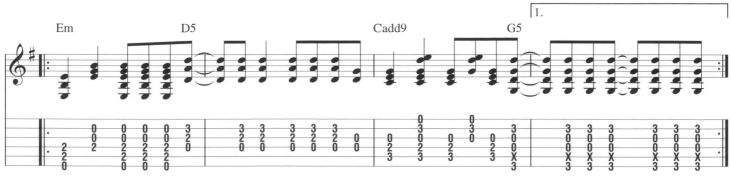

Home

Words and Music by Greg Holden and Drew Pearson

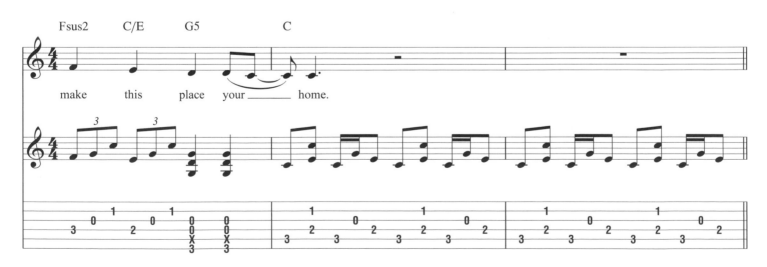

Chorus

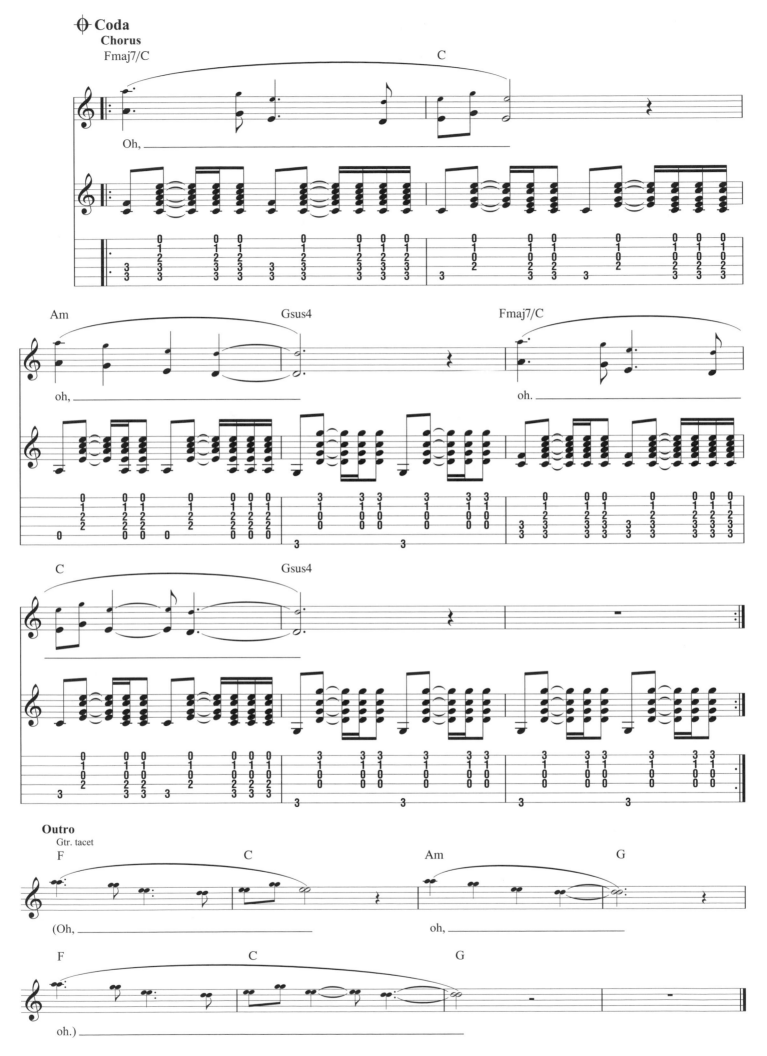

Ho Hey

Words and Music by Jeremy Fraites and Wesley Schultz

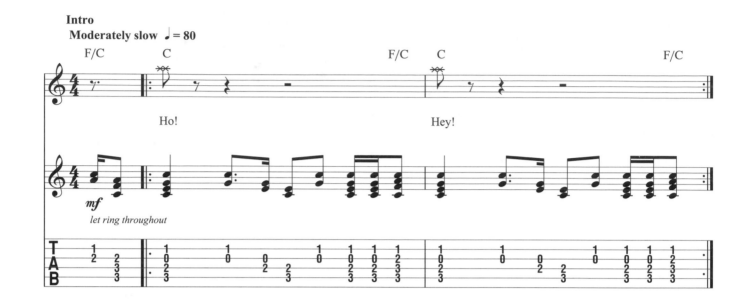

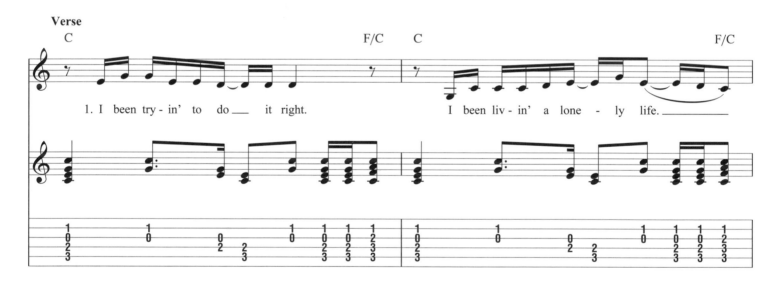

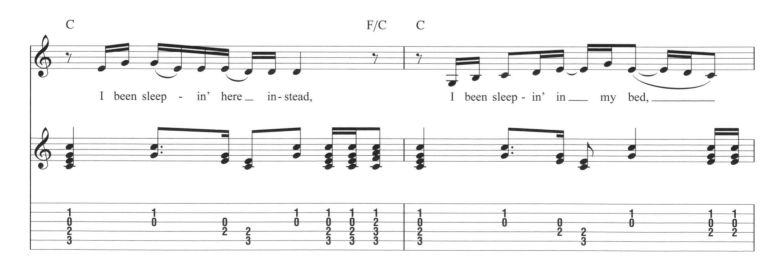

Chorus
Double-time feel

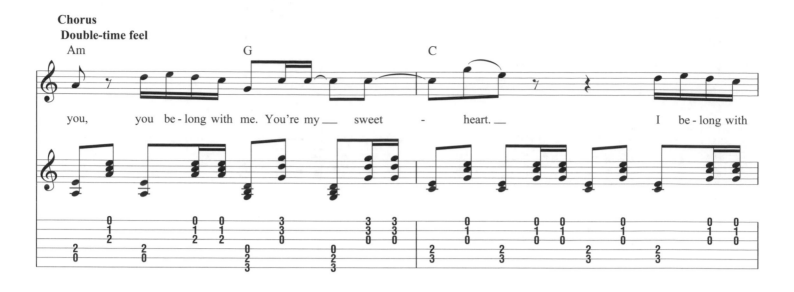

you,   you be-long with me. You're my ___ sweet - heart. ___   I be-long with

Interlude
End double-time feel

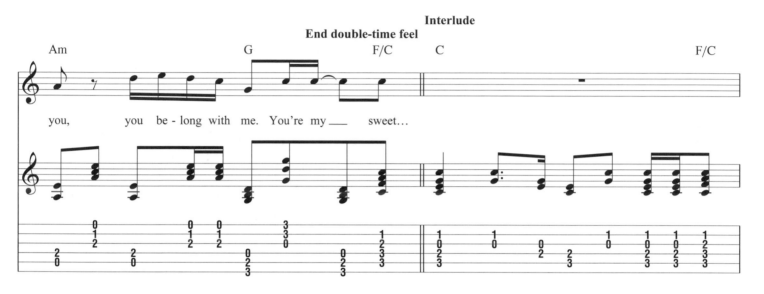

you,   you be-long with me. You're my ___ sweet...

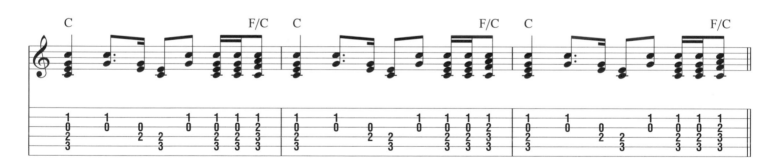

Verse

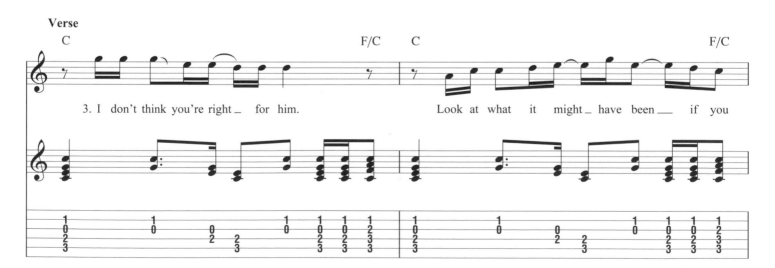

3. I don't think you're right ___ for him.   Look at what it might ___ have been ___ if you

Bridge

Rhythm of Love

Words and Music by Tim Lopez

*To match original recording, place capo at 1st fret.

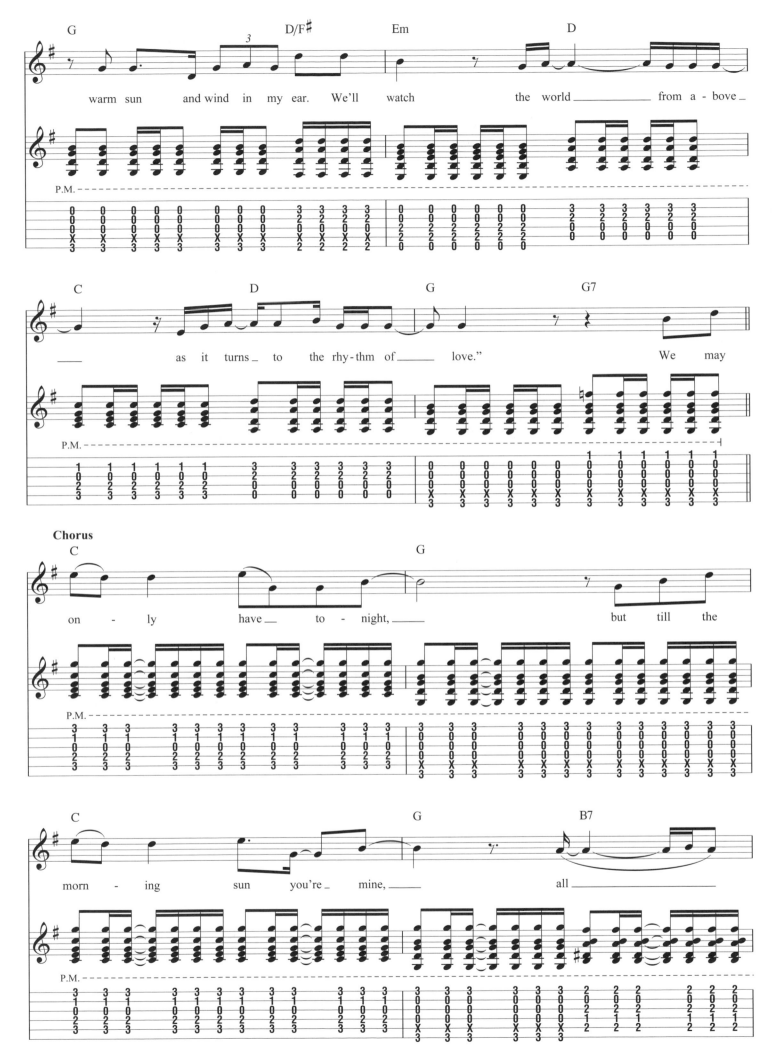

Interlude

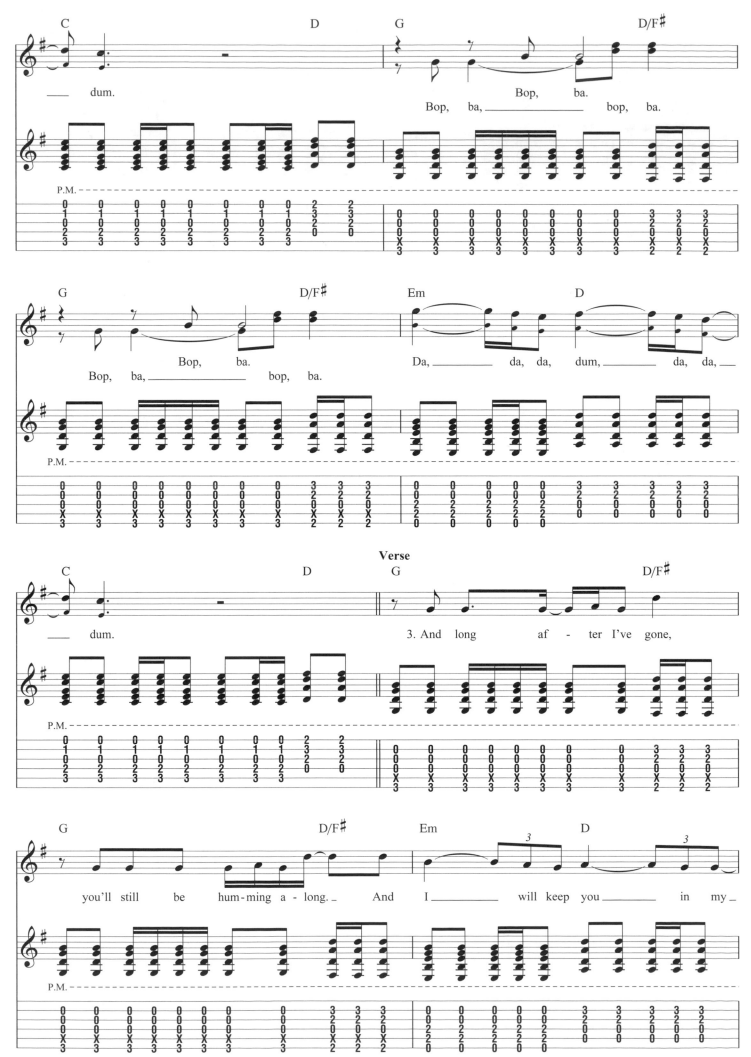

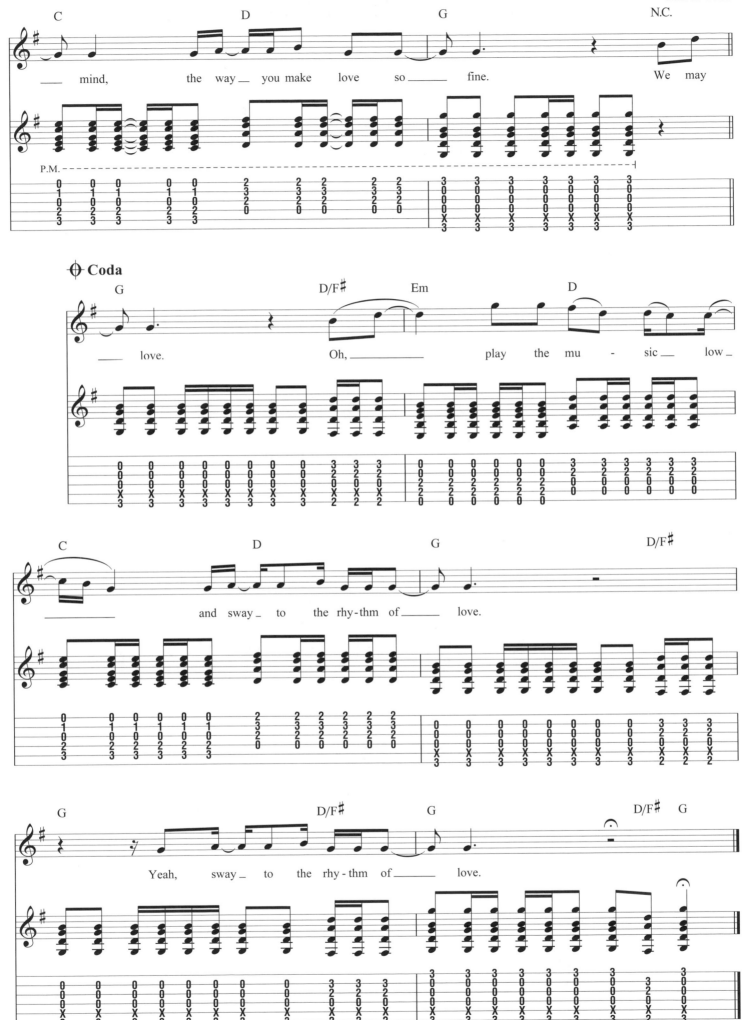

Rolling in the Deep

Words and Music by Adele Adkins and Paul Epworth

it to the beat. _____ We could-'ve had it

Tears are gon-na fall, __ roll-ing in the deep.) __ roll-ing in the deep.) __

Bridge

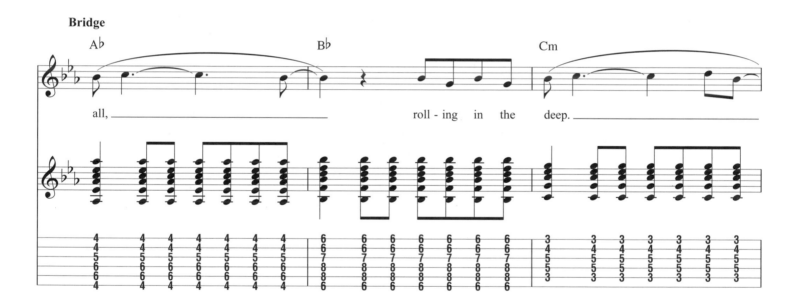

all, _____ roll-ing in the deep. _____

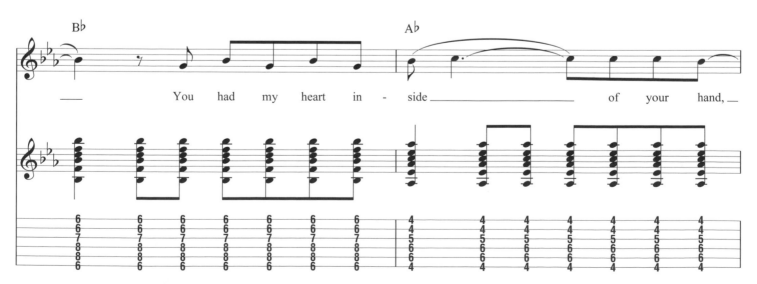

___ You had my heart in - side _____ of your hand, __

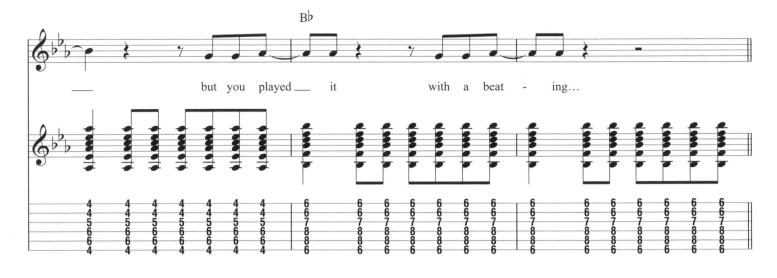

but you played ___ it with a beat - ing...

Breakdown-Verse

Gtr. tacet

N.C.

Throw your ___ soul _____ through ev - er - y o - pen door,

count your ___ bless - ings to find what you look for. Turn my ___ sor - rows

in - to treas-ured gold. You'll pay me ___ back in kind, and reap just what you've sown. ___

Pre-Chorus

Cm   B♭   A♭

We could -'ve had it all. _____

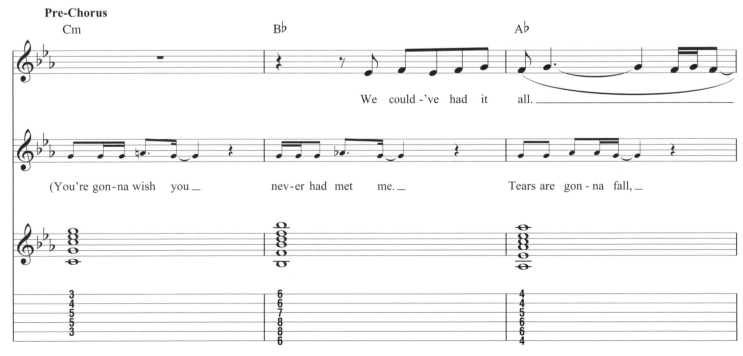

(You're gon-na wish you ___ nev-er had met me. ___ Tears are gon-na fall, ___

The Scientist

Words and Music by Guy Berryman, Jon Buckland, Will Champion and Chris Martin

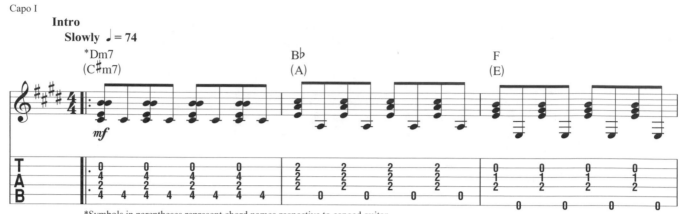

*Symbols in parentheses represent chord names respective to capoed guitar.
Symbols above reflect actual sounding chords. Capoed fret is "0" in tab.

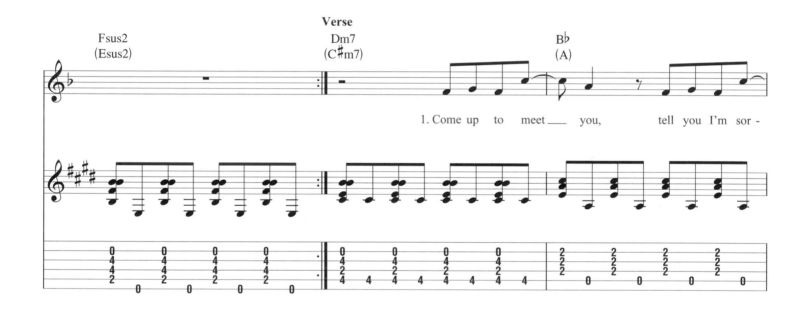

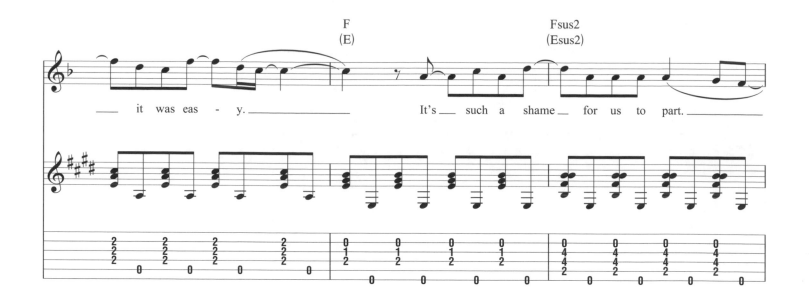

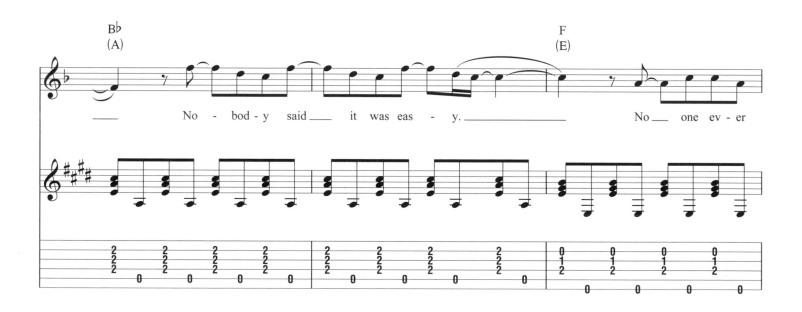

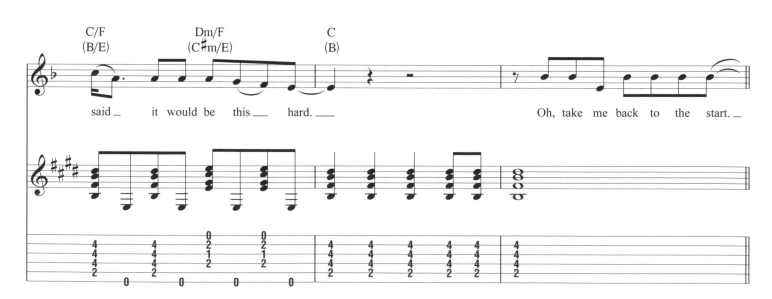

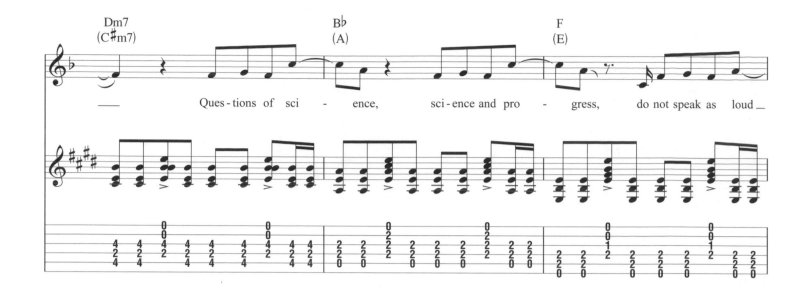

Ques-tions of sci - ence, sci-ence and pro - gress, do not speak as loud __

__ as my heart. _____ Tell me you love __ me, come back and haunt __

__ me, oh, when I rush _____ to the start. _____ Run-nin' in cir -

Let Her Go

Words and Music by Michael David Rosenberg

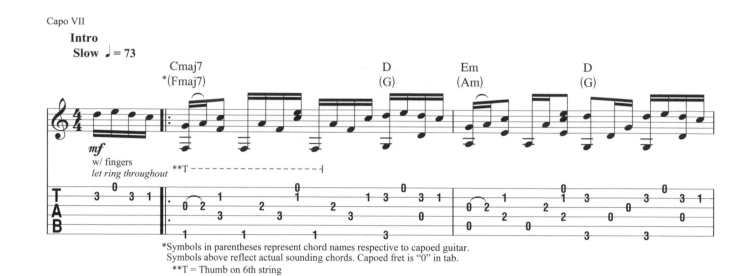

*Symbols in parentheses represent chord names respective to capoed guitar.
Symbols above reflect actual sounding chords. Capoed fret is "0" in tab.
**T = Thumb on 6th string

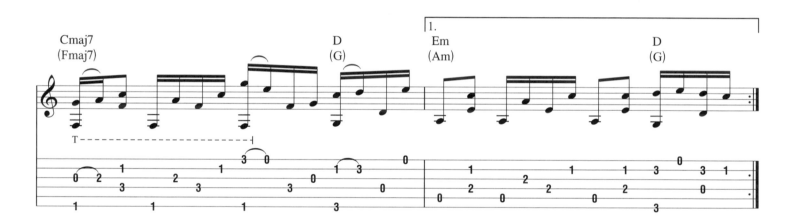

Well, you on-ly need the light when it's burn-ing low. On-ly miss the

sun when it starts to snow. _ On - ly know you love her when you let her go.

On - ly know _ you've been high when you're feel - ing low. On - ly hate the

road when you're miss - ing home. _ On - ly know you love her when you let her go.

Interlude

And you let her go. ___

w/ pick

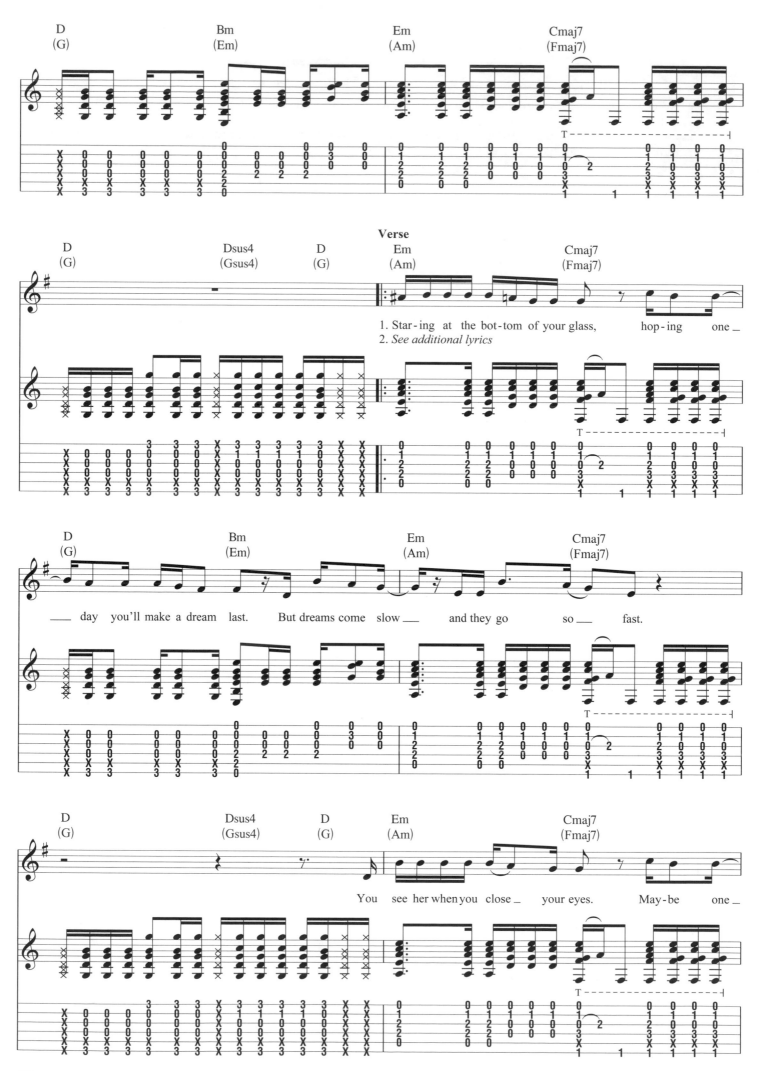

1. Star-ing at the bot-tom of your glass, hop-ing one

2. *See additional lyrics*

day you'll make a dream last. But dreams come slow and they go so fast.

You see her when you close your eyes. May-be one

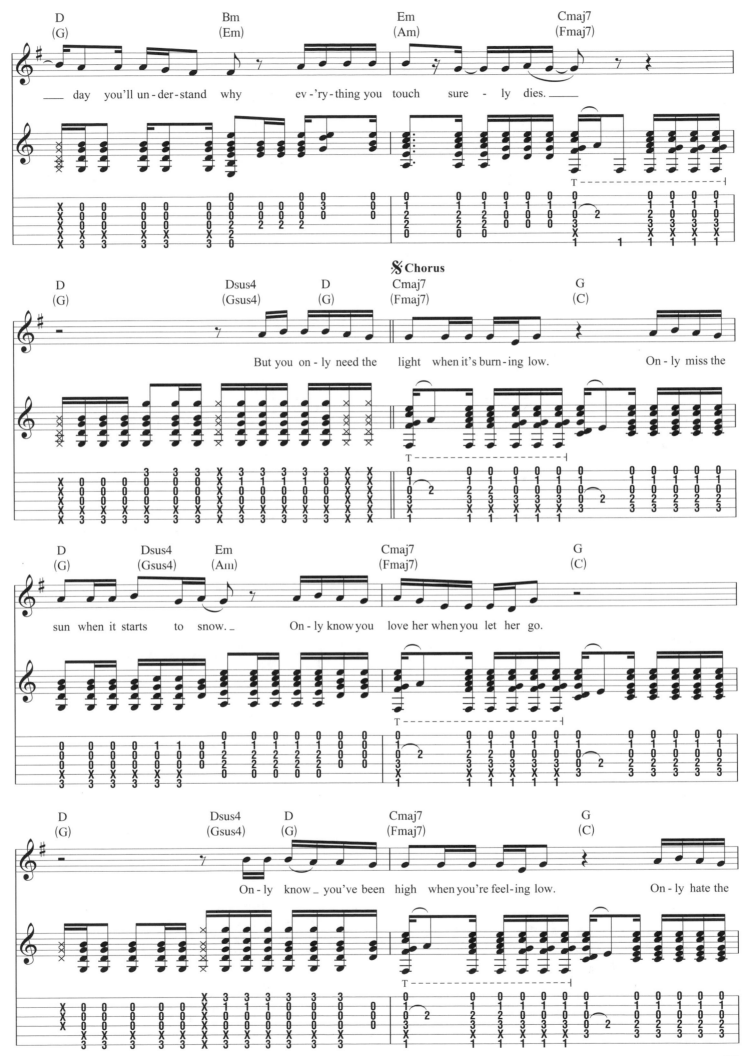

Chorus

road when you're miss-ing home. ___ On - ly know you love her when you let her go.

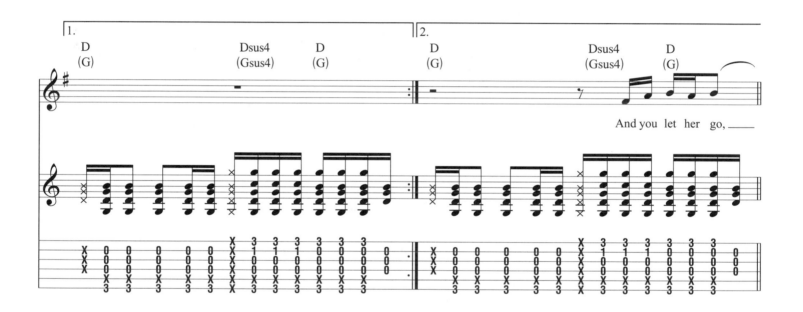

And you let her go, ___

Interlude

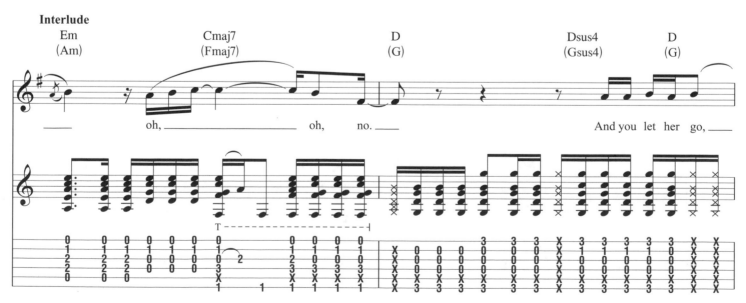

oh, ___ oh, no. ___ And you let her go, ___

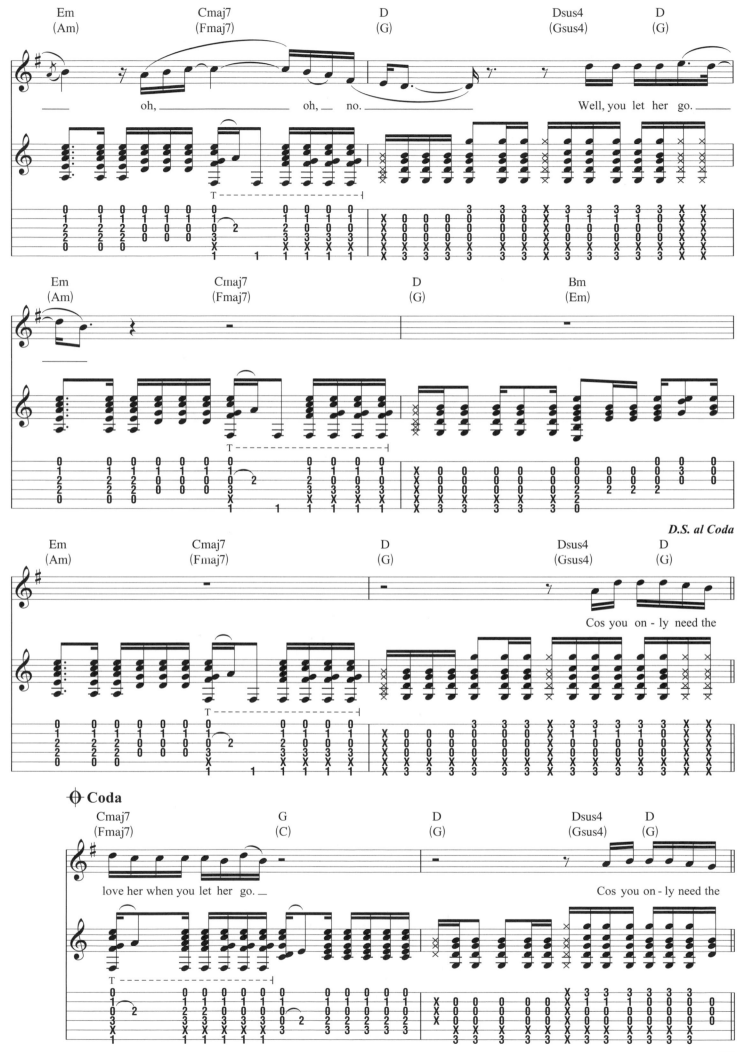

Outro-Chorus

light when it's burn-ing low. On - ly miss the sun when it starts to snow. _ On - ly know you

love her when you let her go. On - ly know _ you've been

high when you're feel-ing low. On - ly hate the road when you're miss - ing home. _ On - ly know you

love her when you let her go. And you let her go. _____

Additional Lyrics

2. Staring at the ceiling in the dark.
   Same old empty feeling in your heart,
   Cos love comes slow and it goes so fast.
   Well, you see her when you fall asleep.
   But never to touch and never to keep,
   Cos you loved her too much and you dived too deep.
   Well, you only need the…